THE ULTIMATE GUIDE

HOW TO TRIAN YOUR GIRLFRIEND

British Library Cataloguing in Publication Data:
A catalogue record of this book is available from the British Library

ISBN 978-1977817846

Printed and bound in Great Britain.

CONTENTS

PREFACE

You have taken the first steps to gaining control of your relationship and all future relationships. With this book, you will learn techniques and skills required to understand what creates a healthy, fulfilling relationship and how you as the male and gain and maintain control of your partner

We'll look at relationships from the perspective of qualified individuals within the field of psychology, world famous a Pickup Artists and of course woman themselves.

Everything in here has been tried and tested to work for you to get the 'perfect partner' That being said, like everything of importance, the power contained in these pages can be utilized for both good and evil. I leave it to you, the reader, to be mature enough to utilize this information for your own motivations behind it.

INTRODUCTION

T hroughout this book, you'll find new and unique skills, which you won't find in your typical "relationship expert" book. This is because much of what is contained within this book is not politically correct enough to make it to such places.

I've spent many years researching techniques and skills to develop the 'perfect partner'. An after spending a long time with what's known as the "seduction community", Originally I noticed a definite lack of any and all information regarding long-term relationships. In fact, I began to get the distinct impression that it was almost frowned upon. Maybe this phenomenon was merely the result of a lack of proper information on relationships. Or maybe none of these people actually knew how to foster a real relationship that actually worked.

Although I've certainly had my fun as a result of the things I've learned during my time spent in this underground seduction movement, I've always been more of a relationship kind of guy. I mean, what's not to like about a never-ending the supply of easy, unprotected sex, friendship and fun? Which is exactly what a relationship provides, by the way.

The vast majority of guys who enter into the seduction community actually just want to find a decent girlfriend who they can have fun with, fall in love with, etc. Unfortunately, many lose sight of this original goal in the pursuit of sex with multiple, random women. Many end up falling into a cycle of "validation driven pickup". They derive their self-worth from the number of women they can sleep with. A sad existence indeed.

We have observed many men in our everyday life who have built successful relationships and we have interviewed dozens of famous Pickup Artists (most of which are now in happy, committed long-term relationships).

Long-term relationships are a worthy goal and I can promise you that no matter how painful a breakup may be, the good times you had with that person will always outweigh the bad. Love, as traditionally defined, is and always will be a worthy pursuit.

A FRESH START

At this very point in human history, we are experiencing a great deal of miraculous and amazing change. You should be incredibly excited to be a part of it. I know I am.

Never before in human existence have women been considered our equals. Never before have there been reliable contraceptives available, virtually irradiating the risk of sex for both men and women. Yet in the midst of this awesomeness, we have lost something.

With the feminist movement came a great deal of [much needed] power to women. Literally, for all of human history, women had been repressed and controlled by men. Even today, in some countries, women routinely have their clitoris removed at a very young age. This is done so they will not experience any sexual pleasure. What a wonderful place to live, I'm sure.

It is truly a marvel that we as a modern society have progressed so far as to finally give women the equality and rights they have for so long deserved. But with this new movement came the loss of something special. Something nobody could point out without being labelled sexist. This transitional period was a time of over sensitivity and intense political correctness. Open discussion on this matter was strictly prohibited, to the detriment of society.

Within the last 100 years, women have slowly become more masculine while men have slowly become more feminine. In our drive for equality we have failed to recognize that while men and women are indeed equal, we are still biologically different creatures. We are not identical; especially when it comes to what we are attracted to.

You see, there is a natural polarity of the sexes. There are specific things that we as a species are genetically programmed to be attracted to. Millions of years of human evolution have ensured this. Evolution does not know what political correctness means.

In the midst of this marvellous revolution, we men have forgotten what it means to be men. What we have lost is indeed our sense of usefulness. In the past, women needed men to survive. Our function was to provide security; a function that has since been deemed obsolete. We are now in a state of perpetual limbo, unsure of where we fit into the grand scheme of things. We have lost our way.

In order to understand how you can take back control of your relationship, you must first come to understand how and why you lost control in the first place.

You must first understand that by nature, the male and female sexes are naturally designed to gravitate toward specific masculine/feminine polarities. There are only rare exceptions to this.

By merely getting yourself into a long-term relationship, you have proven that you are in fact attractive to the opposite sex. At some point, you made her feel feminine. All that is required is for you to maintain the natural polarity of the sexes. You simply need to continue behaving in an attractive manner.

Don't worry; we'll be covering that in later chapters.

SELECTING A HIGH-QUALITY GIRLFRIEND

When it comes to women, whatever you do, please do not just "take whatever you can get". The higher your standards are, the easier it will be to actually attract a woman in the first place, believe it or not. This stems from the fact that women are inherently attracted to men of high value, and men of high value have standards. High standards.

Regardless of whether or not you currently have a girlfriend, I want you to get out a piece of paper, a pen and answer the following questions:

- What are the important qualities you desire in a girlfriend?

- Why are those things important to you?

- List a number of reservations you have when it comes to entering into a long-term relationship. In other words, what are your fears?

- If somebody wrote a list of things about you that fit their needs in a partner, what would they be?

- What do you most enjoy in life?

- What do you most appreciate about yourself?

I know those questions are "deep", but they are absolutely necessary if you are to select a quality long-term girlfriend. Realize that the above questions are not so much about your girlfriend, as they are about YOU. You must know yourself before you can ever hope to trust your own judgment enough to select a long-term mate (or even to stay with your current girlfriend).

THE ANSWERS

You need to know what you want in a girl before you even consider getting yourself into a long-term relationship. Answer the questions before you continue reading on, else you will only be doing yourself a disservice.

Knowing exactly what you want in a woman will only serve to make you more attractive. Women want a man who knows what he wants in life, which includes knowing what qualities he looks for in a woman. Only high-value men are selective and the rest have no standards beyond "nice tits and a nice ass".

Now, don't get me wrong. Nice tits and a nice ass are important to me. I'm a guy and I have my desires. I make no apologies for that. However, a girl with nice tits and a nice ass with absolutely nothing going on upstairs will not result in a satisfying long-term relationship. I know this from personal experience.

Which brings me to…

COMPATIBILITY

I'm generally not a huge fan of "traditional" relationship advice. It usually encourages overly submissive behaviour on the man's part, which I strongly disagree with. However, when it comes to the age-old advice on being compatible, I would definitely have to agree.

Opposites do not attract. I believe that advice originally stems from the observation of sweet and innocent women fawning over bad boys like James Dean. Women will always be attracted to masculine men, regardless of their common interests. There is no denying this.

However, if you are to have any long-term success (in terms of happiness at least), you need to be with a woman you enjoy for reasons other than physical beauty. Like everything in life, that shiny, pretty face will eventually fade away, leaving what behind? And even if you don't end up growing old together, you will eventually become desensitized by her beauty. You'll grow tired of it, and desire a fresh face.

Your relationship needs to be based on more than just physical lust. There truly has to be a strong friendship behind the scenes; and as much as I distrust traditional relationship advice (for men at least), I wholeheartedly stand by this old piece of wisdom.

COMMON PASSION

Wondering why I made your list what you are passionate about in life? It's simple really. You and your potential girlfriend should share a common passion. This truly is one of those oh so obvious yet oh so overlooked things. So many guys just jump into a relationship with either the first hot chick that shows a bit of interest in him or the first woman who presents herself as a challenge.

Don't fall into that trap. Figure out what you have fun doing in life and find a woman who shares many of those same passions as possible. Even if it's just one, it will be more than enough, considering most couples share a total of zero passions. This really is important because you don't ever want to change who you are as a person just to fit into your girlfriend's reality.

Now, if you already have a girlfriend, and you think you don't share any particular passion, I recommend you try to get her involved in any hobbies or other interests you have. Suck her into your reality and make sure she has a great time in it.

THE MOST NECESSARY FACTOR CONCERNING RELATIONSHIPS

The most important thing to know when getting into a long-term relationship is that the deeper you both progress into the relationship, the more significant "inner game" becomes.

Inner game is your collective beliefs, attitudes and generally how you view yourself as a person. It adversely affects your frame and your behaviour.

If you sincerely view yourself positively, as a prize and as a man of high value, you will naturally behave in an attractive manner. If you view yourself negatively and approach the relationship with a "what can I do to make her like me more and keep her interested" attitude, you will consequently behave in all the wrong ways.

I've put a lot of thought into why men do things for women and I think I've come to a pretty solid conclusion. It all comes down to your underlying intentions.

Guys do and say things (like spending money, saying "I love you", complimenting, etc) for two main reasons:

#1. To gain her acceptance and approval.

Men will buy their girlfriend diamonds, shoes, clothes, expensive dinners – you name it all as a means to buy her affections. Men will say "I love you" much too soon in a relationship because they want their girlfriend to love them back, just like when they buy her material possessions so she will like them more. It's an act of needy desperation; one in which women (and men for that matter) can smell a mile away. In fact, you've probably experienced this yourself.

#2. Because they genuinely care…

…about the others happiness and the act of giving makes them happy. Have you ever given a gift to your mother or a close friend just to see the look on their face? And when their eyes lit up, you felt all warm and fuzzy inside? The act of giving the gift actually made you happy! That's the place you should be coming from whenever you do somethe thing for your girlfriend. You don't even have to say it she will just know.

Frame everything you do for your girlfriend as a gift from you to her. Every time you're going to do something for her, stop first and ask yourself what your underlying intentions are.

Is it to gain her acceptance and approval, or because seeing her happy makes you all warm and fuzzy inside? Whether you're spending money on her, saying "I love you", driving her around, or whatever: Make sure you're doing it because it makes you happy to see her happy.

Never do something for her because you think she's losing interest in you or because you want her to care for you more. I promise you it will have the complete opposite effect.

TRANSITIONING INTO A LONG TERM RELATIONSHIP

Many of you who bought this book will undoubtedly be in a relationship currently, in which case you can choose to skip over this section. However, many of you will have bought this to prepare yourselves for any future relationships you may enter into. Smart move.

Fortunately for you, transitioning into a long-term relationship is very simple. Women are hard-wired to want a relationship with a man who is providing her with frequent, good sex. All that is required is for you to let the woman worry about the transition. It's her job to advance the relationship past casual sex. In other words, she needs to pop the question.

I remember many years ago, I was casually dating this one girl. Although she was very young (eighteen) and was sexually active, she didn't want to have sex with me because as she put it "I've slept with too many guys and I don't want you thinking I'm a slut."

I saw something special in this girl and so I didn't really push her for sex. I could see that it genuinely bothered her and so we chose to pleasure each other in alternative ways, which I actually enjoy more than sex itself, so I could honestly have cared less.

When we finally did end up having sex, (fourth date) she immediately told me that since we had sex we were officially dating and that I had no say in the matter. I think she was only half joking, but nevertheless, I just smiled and said: "I accept". And thus began our relationship.

The point of that story is to highlight the fact that I didn't bother worrying about the "label" we placed on "us". I let her worry about it and she eventually popped the question, even if it was only in a half-joking way. If she wants to be in a relationship with you, she will find a way to bring up the subject eventually.

Now with that said, if you want to make it past the transitional period, you need to behave in a very specific manner directly after sex. This is not the time to roll over and go to sleep, or even worse, act moody and rude toward her. The post-sex cuddle is the most critical transitional period, as it will indicate to the woman whether or not you want

to move things to the next level. If you behave negatively, she will assume you only want sex and she will quickly cut her losses.

What you should be doing after sex:

- Cuddling with her.
- Talking, having fun and laughing together.
- Smiling.
- Being gentle and caressing her.
- Kissing her on the forehead.
- Going out for food.

I don't want you to follow the above like some sort of script. It is just a list of examples to show that post-sex is the time to really be affectionate. It demonstrates that you want an actual long-term relationship and women need to see this behaviour to verify your intentions.

It's also very important to note that the first time you have sex with her, you need to call her the next day. If you fail to do this, she will more than likely feel used and neglected. Her "anti-slut defence" will go up and you'll be fighting an uphill battle from that point on. I recommend you make things easy for yourself and call her the next day if your intentions are indeed to keep her as a long-term girlfriend.

THE SECRET TO LASTING ATTRACTION
MALE/FEMALE POLARITY

Have you ever really liked a girl only to have her slowly lose interest and attraction for you after a few months? Maybe that girl was even in love with you at one point. Were you left wondering "where did I go wrong?"

Do you want to know what the key to long-lasting attraction in a relationship is? I can tell you that it isn't some trick or gimmick. It isn't some line you can feed her. No, it's actually more profound than any of that.

You see, women want to feel feminine and in order for them to really feel feminine, they must be in the presence of a masculine man. The real key to long-lasting attraction is for you to exhibit the traits of a masculine man; to fulfil your natural role of masculinity. Her genetic code demands that she feel feminine when around her mate. The more you can facilitate her feelings of femininity, the stronger her attraction for you will grow over time.

Think back to any failed relationship you may have had in the past. When things started to go wrong, were you acting more and more submissive and your girlfriend more and more dominant? This is indeed why most relationships end. The woman begins to feel masculine and the man begins to feel feminine. This reversal of roles literally kills any and all attraction.

The key to lasting attraction, in short, is a polarization between the sexes. The man assumes the role of dominant leader and the woman assumes the role of submissive follower. As sexist as this all may sound to some, you must realize that it's genetic. This is literally how we are programmed to feel and behave! Evolution doesn't know what it's like to be politically correct.

The great thing about all of this is that you don't need to force your girlfriend into any particular role, one way or the other. In fact, if you try to force submission upon her, your relationship will quickly end. You simply need to focus on fulfilling the role of a mature, masculine man and she will automatically fall into the role of submissive follower. No force or controlling behaviour required!

None of this means you need to transform yourself into an asshole, by the way. Masculinity is not equal to immaturity.

FATHER FRAME

I believe that women are inherently attracted to men who are like their father. Whenever I start dating a new woman, I find myself intently observing her father. Not because I want to change my personality and become like him, but rather to better judge whether or not my new girlfriend and I are a good match.

I am not advocating you become like her father by any means, but rather that you assume the mindset of a protective father. This especially applies when "punishing" her. You must do it because you care about her (it is for her own good) and not out of insecurity and the desire to control her.

Much like any good father (there are plenty of bad ones), you must assume the role of mature mentor. You must become her strong leadership. Her rock.

Lead from a position of love.

TRAITS OF AN IRRESISTIBLE MALE

LEADER

Women naturally want to be lead by a strong man. They want to be taken in hand and shown the way. I could go on and on as to why this is evolutionarily accurate, but I will spare you the unnecessary details. Right now, the only important thing you must know is how to properly lead a woman.

For starters, be the one to make plans. Next time you're planning a date, know where you are going, how you will be getting there and at what time. Take it a step further and tell her what you want her to wear. "Baby, I think that little black dress is super sexy. Wear it tonight." You'll even find that most women will ask you what they should wear. I never even noticed this until I started telling them what I wanted to see on them. I think it is their way of pushing us to lead them. I doubt they even realize it themselves.

DECISIVE

Knowing what you want in life and going for it is yet another very attractive masculine quality. This trait really compliments leadership, because you have to be decisive in order to effectively lead in the first place.

Next time your girlfriend asks you "what do you want to do tonight baby?" don't respond with "I don't know what do you want to do?" Just take the initiative and throw something out there. "We're going to go for coffee and then wherever that takes us." Just say anything. Don't think it has to be something fabulous. As long as you say something, you're on the right path.

Even when you're at the movies, know which movie you want to go see. You don't have to fight with her overseeing a particular show, but at least know what it is you personally want to see. If she disagrees, recommend a second movie, etc.

Decisiveness is a quality that develops the more you use it. I used to be a horribly indecisive person. I worked on my problem for a long time and now I'm proud to say I can make decisions on the fly. I finally realized that: "When you come to a fork in the road, take it."

SELF ASSURED

Be assertive, be assertive, be assertive! To be self-assured is to not compromise your own opinions to better fit others. You need to believe in the power of you. Let go of the fear of being judged by your girlfriend and speak your mind more. You don't have to be an ass about it either; you just need to be firm and know where you stand.

Scenario: You're out shopping with your girlfriend.

The Wrong Way:

You: I really like this shirt.

Her: Really? I don't. It looks like something a
bum would wear.

You: Yeah. I guess you're right. I won't get it then.

The Right Way:

You: I really like this shirt.

Her: Really? I don't. It looks like something a
bum would wear.

You: *you put a big smile on your face and hold
up the shirt* Well I guess I'm just going to have to
get it for sure now.

wink

You see, the "right way" example demonstrates that you
follow your own sense of internal validation. You
liked the shirt and so you bought it. Women respect this
type of masculine attitude immensely.

Furthermore, in the above "right way" example, you were
funny and played it off as a joke/tease. You didn't start a

fight over it or turn it into a "dominance struggle". You just played it off as silly.

SELF-CONTROLLED

Being masculine has a lot to do with maturity and maturity is all about being responsible. Imagine yourself driving down the highway with your girlfriend, only to come to a traffic jam. A bloody long one too. You respond by immediately cursing at the drivers in front of you, laying on the horn and generally just acting pissed off. Now, how mature is that?

Your lady is going to lose respect for you right then and there. Instead, you should take the opportunity to have some fun with her. Joke around about something, talk about all the fun stuff you plan on doing that week. Get her to give you a blowjob. If that doesn't calm you down, I don't know what will.

About a year ago, I took a past girlfriend on a "date" to the local park. We arrived at around 12:30 AM. It was the middle of the night. We ended up just running around, rolling in the wet grass and "played" on the slide. We basically just goofed around and got to know each other better for two hours.

At around 2:30 AM it started raining, so we ran back to my car. Me being the amazingly intelligent guy that I apparently forgot to shut the lights off. The battery was dead and it was 2:30 in the morning. Who would the hell be around to give me a boost?

I was pretty pissed at first, but then I decided to take this impossibly unsmooth situation and turn it into something awesome. I looked at my girlfriend, licked my lips and grabbed her by the collar. "Get over here" I whispered, with a seductive look in my eyes. I pulled her in close and could feel her heart beating fast.

We had wild sex for three hours in my back seat. After that, I put in a really corny CD with love songs (how did that get in my deck?) and cuddled for another hour or two. She drew hearts on the steam covered back windows.

When daylight came and everyone was off to work, I told my girlfriend to go ask random guys in a seductive voice if they would give her a boost. The first guy she asked accepted eagerly.

Most guys would have just flipped out and ruined the whole night for themselves and their girl.

MODEST

For some reason, modesty is often equated with weakness. This could not be any further from the truth. In fact, it is the man with true inner strength who can disqualify himself and resist the urge to let others place him on a pedestal. Keep in mind that being modest is not about putting yourself down; it is about not letting others place you atop a pedestal.

Many of us are so under appreciated that whenever anyone says something nice about us, we immediately agree and even take it as an opportunity to start bragging. Don't let yourself fall into this trap. Sincerely thank the person for their compliment and move on.

APPROVAL GIVING

We men are pretty touchy with our approval. For some odd reason, we feel as though it's needy or validation seeking, when in fact it is anything but. Wayne Elise (a famous Pickup Artist) describes approval as a sort of currency. If you never spend it, it's the same as having none.

If you have no value, you cannot give value away. It's a simple concept really. Men of power and influence are never afraid to give genuine praise and appreciation for others. They have "value", they know it and they are not afraid to share it.

Take Donald Trump for example. Regardless of whether you like him or not, he is the most approval giving an example of an alpha male I can think of. If you've ever seen him in an interview, no matter what, he is always going on about how awesome everyone around him is.

"Yes, I know Jen. I met her briefly during dinner at the Ritz once. She's a beautiful girl. Very intelligent and well mannered. I love her sense of style too. Just marvellous."

Women don't like men who continually take approval from them. In other words, men who put down and make fun of them. They know it comes from a place of insecurity and a desire to lower everyone else to their own level. Note that I'm not talking about "teasing" here. I highly encourage playful teasing.

Approval can be extremely addictive. Think of it as your own personal drug that you feed the woman in your life. I mean, it's actually much more effective than sticking a nicotine patch on her arm while she sleeps and removing it in the morning, so she'll associate the craving for nicotine with you. (If somebody emails me saying that didn't work, I'm going to pee my pants!)

But seriously, your approval works in much the same way. You want her associating good feelings with you, and approval is exactly what that provides. As a people, we are generally very underappreciated, so when somebody is unafraid to show genuine appreciation for them and what they can do, it feels very good.

In fact, as you will come to read in later sections of this book, approval is one of the main ways in which you will go about "training" your girlfriend to love, appreciate and respect you.

AMBITIOUS

Ambition is unbelievably sexy to women. It is one of the ultimate attraction switches.

You see, women don't particularly want men who are wealthy; they want men who are ambitious. In other words, wealthy men are attractive to women not because they are wealthy, but because their wealth demonstrates ambition.

It is true even today that the most ambitious men are the most successful. They have survival value, and women are hardcoded to pick up on this. They will stay with a man who is ambitious, over a man who is wealthy and not ambitious.

I'm going to venture a guess that millions of years ago, the most ambitious cavemen were also the most successful.

They led their tribes, brought home the best food, received favouritism from other cavemen, etc, etc. Their ambition paid out huge dividends to the women they eventually mated with.

Now with that said, you must realize that ambition isn't something that can be faked. You need to actually be ambitious, to one degree or another.

It's easy to fake ambition with stories when you first meet a woman, but when you're in a long-term relationship, actions speak louder than words. Women will judge you not by the grandiose stories you tell them, but by the things you demonstrate via your actions.

Keep in mind that ambition is not all about wealth. You can be a very ambitious hippie if you really want. You

know, hippies save trees and stuff. That's their ambition!
And a pretty damn good one I might add.

What's important is that you set goals for yourself and
strive for them; just like the leaders of Green Peace or
even the filthy rich executives at Exxon. Both extremes
have an ambition that gives their lives purpose.

Make your life goals known to your girlfriend. In fact,
encourage her to share her own life goals and aspirations
with you. Figure out what you are passionate about in
life, what your life purpose is. Knowing these things will
only serve to better your life in more ways than just
making your girlfriend extremely attracted to you.

RELATIONSHIP KILLERS: WHY LADIES DUMP MEN

APPROVAL SEEKING BEHAVIOUR

Constantly looking to your girlfriend for approval is attraction death.

Being externally validation oriented is the hallmark of a man with low

self-esteem. As you know, men of high value have very high confidence and equally high self-esteem.

If you're one of those guys who's always looking for his girlfriend to see if it's okay for him to do this or that, you really need to look into changing that bad habit. Women are genetically preprogrammed to want a man who is self-reliant. Be that man!

CONTROLLING BEHAVIOUR

For some reason, when men get into relationships, they start to view their girlfriend as property. They will attempt to control who their girlfriend is with, ask her where she is at 24/7 and generally act very controlling. This is the completely wrong attitude to have. You see, men who attempt to control their girlfriends are really doing so from a place of insecurity.

Perhaps they feel threatened by other guys, or they want her attention focused solely on them and not on her other girlfriends. In any case, this behaviour is needy, weak and far from masculine. It demonstrates to your girlfriend that you are threatened, and only low-value men feel threatened. Period.

Scenario: You're at a club and your girlfriend starts dancing with another guy.

THE WRONG WAY:

You immediately jump into controlling boyfriend mode, march over to her with a look of stone on your face and mouth through your teeth: "what do you think you're doing?" Maybe you even grab her hand, pull her to the side of the dance floor and demand she not dance with other guys.

THE RIGHT WAY:

You're cool about it. As long as she's not making out with him, it's no sweat off your back. She's just having fun dancing with some dude who is nothing compared to you. Who she dances with is her own business. You know that if she ends up doing something stupid like making out with him, then she's clearly not worth it and you'll dump her immediately. This is you testing her loyalty. It's your way of filtering out the worthless bitches.

Examples of men trying to control their girlfriends:

- Insist she not goes to parties and bars without him present.

- Follow their girlfriend around and generally hover over her while at these parties, bars and clubs.

- Try to stop her from hanging out with other men.

- Ask her a million and one questions:

"Where were you last night?"

"Who was that guy I saw you talking with before?" "Who are you hanging out with this weekend?"

He who is the least controlling controls the relationship. Write that out one hundred times if you have to.

JEALOUSY

Jealous and controlling behaviour goes hand in hand. This is because when feeling jealous, men will often try to control the situation in an attempt to make those feelings go away. We're always trying to fix things, us men.

Scenario: Your girlfriend tells you she's hanging out with an old friend from high school.

THE WRONG WAY:

You automatically go into jealous boyfriend mode and start asking her a million questions. "Who is this guy?", "Do you like him?", "What are you guys doing?"

Your girlfriend reassures you that he's just an old friend from high school and you have nothing to worry about. You continue to act pissed off for the rest of the day.

THE RIGHT WAY:

You're calm, relaxed and cool about it. You act as though it's no big deal. "That's awesome babe. Here, let me help you pick out something to wear." You have the mentality that this other guy will only make you look good; which he probably will. Not to mention the fact she's probably telling the truth and he really is just an old friend.

The cold truth is that nothing kills relationships more so than jealousy. Hands down, bar none. Jealousy stems from a place of fear and insecurity. In other words, it turns you into a weak, sad excuse for a man. I cannot stress to you enough how unattractive jealousy is to women.

In fact, if faced with the option of either acting jealous or doing nothing, always do nothing. No amount of insecure bitching on your part will ever keep her from talking to guys, hanging out with other friends and so forth.

Women are only attracted to men who value themselves highly and I'll tell you right now, if you place a significant amount of importance on yourself, you won't be acting jealous, to begin with. You simply will not feel threatened by anything or anybody.

You need to adopt the attitude that since you're such a great guy, other guys will only make you look good.

Having a relaxed, unworried attitude about the above situation communicates to your girlfriend that you are secure in yourself. You are so secure in yourself that you would never even think to view this other guy as a threat. Additionally, it communicates that you trust her; something both women and men alike places a significant amount of importance on.

"If he doesn't trust me, why am I even with him?" is what she'll be thinking.

It's also important to note that if you believe your girlfriend is purely dancing with other guys just to make you jealous, you should consider the possibility she is not emotionally mature enough for a real long-term relationship. See chapter #11 for more information on punishing bad behaviour.

CLINGINESS

You are "clingy" when you overstay your welcome. Like every "relationship killer", clinginess also comes from a place of insecurity. No surprise there.

Spending time apart is a very important aspect of maintaining a healthy relationship. The feeling of butterflies and knots in your stomach will quickly vanish if you smother each other. Your girlfriend doesn't want you to be glued to her every single day, day in and day out. It doesn't mean she's a horrible person; it simply means she's human.

The concept of supply and demand is alive and well when applied to human relationships. Take diamonds for example diamonds are valuable because they are rare. If you could walk outside your house and pick up a handful whenever you wanted them, they would be completely worthless. Common sense, right? Well, yes, but not when applied to relationships. For most men who fall in love, the urge to be around their significant other is unbearable. Common sense goes straight out the window. You need to control that urge and give her space.

Did you know that diamonds are actually a lot more plentiful than most people think? The supply of diamonds is artificially controlled by the market. They know that if they let a flood of diamonds into jewellery stores, their value would drop dramatically. Suddenly, we no longer view diamonds as valuable because they are so cheap; much like we place extremely little value on dirt.

Have you ever heard the saying "familiarity breeds contempt"? Well, it's actually false. The more time you spend with somebody, the stronger the bond between you grows. I must sound like I'm contradicting myself here. Here I am telling you that you can't be glued to your girlfriend 24/7 and yet the more you are around somebody, the stronger your bond grows.

LETS EXPLAIN:

If you have a girlfriend and you suddenly cut off all contact with her and see her twice a week, you're going to get dumped. She will assume you no longer care about her and thus begin searching for a more suitable mate. The goal here isn't to ignore her and come across as a complete jerk. That would be about as effective as camping outside her house.

Like many of the concepts explored in this book, you need to find balance. I'd recommend quality time spent with your girlfriend a few times per week. Remember: quality over quantity is key. If it so happens that you're spending lots of quality time with your girlfriend, then forget what I said about supply and demand. The mere fact that you are both having loads of fun together circumvents everything.

The main goal of making yourself more scarce is so you can focus on quality time over quantity. Making yourself scarce and spending little amounts of low-quality time with your girlfriend is even worse than loads of low-quality time, believe it or not. I'll say it again: focus on quality over quantity.

I'd actually recommend spending lots of quality time with your girlfriend, but I don't because I know it's unreasonable and for the most part unattainable. You would experience burnout and naturally start to lower the amount of quality time you spend together, increasing the amount of low-quality time. It's human nature and there is no way around it. Therefore, it is much more effective to focus on a moderate amount of quality time with your girlfriend.

Remember, when I say to be scarce, I don't mean disappear; I mean to keep it within moderation. If there were a scale from 1 to 10, 1 being completely scarce and 10 being around her constantly, 3 4 is where you would want to be.

ONE-UPPING

A problem some guys have is they always feel the need to "one-up" everyone around them, including their girlfriends. I had a friend like this once. No matter what, he always had to be better at everything. He was compelled by an overinflated, insecure ego to compete with everyone. He needed to prove himself constantly. To me, this type of behaviour is utterly insecure.

Don't try to "one-up" your girlfriend. If she succeeds at something or displays higher value to you, congratulate her and let her know you're damn impressed! You don't have to always make yourself look better than her. It shows insecurity. You need to be comfortable with yourself, weaknesses and all. A woman will respect a man much more if he accepts his weaknesses, as opposed to one who bitterly tries to overcompensate for any and all deficiencies.

Remember how I said the most important thing you can do when dealing with people is to give away your approval, while not seeking theirs? Well, that applies perfectly to this scenario.

ARGUING

Arguing conveys lower status, plain and simple. This is especially true if you're the one picking the fight. Like any other behaviour, you can either choose to engage in it or not; and when it comes to arguing, you must choose not to engage in it. You are above petty arguments. Simply tell her in a calm tone of voice that you believe the argument is silly, and that it can be dealt with in a mature manner.

Women are much more emotional than us men. Therefore, when in an argument, it is far more effective to change her mood (or simply walk away), rather than logic her to death with why she is wrong and you are right. It literally doesn't matter to her! If the topic of argument is entirely silly and truly not worth discussing, try to reframe it in a playful light. Tease her and call it silly, then give her a pat on the head and a kiss on the forehead.

Based on the fact that men are more logic oriented, if you're ever disagreeing with your girlfriend on something and don't fully understand your position on the issue, take a step back and tell her you to need to gather your thoughts before you proceed. Think things over until you are clear on where you stand; only then will you come back to it.

In the heat of the moment, you won't be able to effectively convey the way you truly feel. Women are much better at dealing with "in the moment" heated verbal battles than their male counterparts. You will more than likely get swept away in the heat of things, and totally mess everything up for yourself. When do men ever win arguments?

You must take the attitude and belief that you are above arguing and that doing such things is completely silly.

ISOLATION

Just like being "clingy" will kill attraction, being isolated from each other for long periods of time will just as easily ruin an otherwise strong relationship. I'll go out on a limb here and admit to you all that this has been the number one killer of all my past failed relationships. It all came down to me not having enough time to invest in my girlfriend. As a result, the opportunity for intimacy was greatly lacking and we just didn't spend any quality time together. Although everything else was great, this deficiency alone caused a chain reaction resulting in the collapse of many strong relationships.

BUILDING AN APPEALING LIFESTYLE

HAVE A LIFE OTHER THAN YOUR GIRLFRIEND

Once in a relationship, many guys will eventually start to drift away from their friends as well as any other activities they once enjoyed. It is very important for you to focus on your own life and not let your girlfriend become your world. Women are attracted to guys who have purpose-driven lives. Your girlfriend will simply not respect you if you value her much more than your own progress in life.

What is it you enjoy doing in life? Perhaps you enjoy working out at the gym, playing tennis, drinking with the guys and watching ESPN on Sundays? If so, you must not stop doing those things just to please your girlfriend. Value yourself as much as you value her. If you are willing to compromise than so should she. My point is, you need to have a life that doesn't involve your girlfriend.

Keep yourself busy with your other life endeavours and she will respect you for that. The man who aimlessly flails about life never knowing what to do with himself, hopelessly clinging to his girlfriend, is very unattractive.

Again, I would like to stress that you do not take this to the extreme. Extremes of any kind are bad. They're bad when it comes to religion, politics, economics and relationships. So, when I say to have a life other than your girlfriend, I mean to do so within reason. If your girlfriend thinks you care little about her, she will leave you. The women who enjoy men who constantly ignore them have major issues and are not emotionally healthy. It's best you stay away from these women from the very beginning.

CREATING BOUNDARIES
DEFINING YOUR BOUNDARIES

Every healthy relationship needs to have clearly defined boundaries. What those boundaries end up being complete depends on you and your own values and self-respect.

You need to sit down and seriously think about what behaviour you will and will not tolerate. Will you give your girlfriend a second chance if she cheats on you? Will you allow her to treat you poorly and boss you around? Can she get away with only taking from the relationship and never giving?

I hope the answer to those questions is obvious. If you're a normal self-respecting human being, you want her to be loyal, you want her treating you like the amazing guy you are and you want her contributing just as much to the relationship as you.

In fact, the minute you truly expect to be treated in all the right ways is the very minute you are treated in all the right ways.

Boundaries must be set at the very beginning of the relationship. That is why you must sit down and actively write out what it is you will and will not tolerate when it comes to your girlfriend's behaviour. You must set these boundaries and you must stick to them no matter what.

It is not enough to merely set these boundaries, you must set consequences for when they are crossed. Some of these boundaries will be crossed at various points of your relationship. Know this. Accept it.

If you tell your girlfriend you do not tolerate cheating, and she cheats on you, you need to have the power and self-respect to end the relationship right then and there. If she acts bitchy toward you, you must have the power to tell her you are not impressed with her behaviour and that you find it unattractive. If she is not contributing to the relationship in any positive way, you must have the power to make your feelings known to her. She must understand that you value your dignity just as much as you value your relationship with her.

I want you to get that pen and paper back out and make a list of your boundaries now. Remember that these are things you care about and not things you feel you necessarily should care about. The more honest you are with yourself the better.

What behaviour will you simply not tolerate?

Make your list now. Do not read any further until you do so.

KEEPING BOUNDARIES "OPEN"

Once you've set your relationships boundaries and know damn well what you will and will not tolerate when it comes to your girlfriend's behaviour, you must keep those boundaries open. That's right, she is free to cross them!

The boundaries we set are not of a controlling nature. We don't control her and demand she not cross the line. Our boundaries are to be completely open and crossable. She must know and understand that you will allow her to cross said boundaries, but she must also fear your disappointment and disapproval. Let me repeat that for impact: she must fear your disappointment and disapproval.

Take teenagers for example. They have a reputation for being "rebellious". I'd venture to guess that the most rebellious of all teenagers are the most repressed and controlled. It is human nature to resist (and resent) that which attempts to control us, as we by nature desire freedom and independence. Hence, those teenagers who are repressed by their parents resist and overcompensate by doing "rebellious" things to proclaim their liberty.

Of course, this cycle of rebellion is vicious. The more these teenagers rebel, the more their parents attempt to control them and the more the teenager's rebel. You get the picture. I bet you can even relate to that analogy, as I

know I certainly can. How many of you were rebellious
to one extent or another and why? Think about it.

What scenario do you think would be more
effective?

You're 13 and go out binge drinking for the first time.
Wow, that was fun! You proceed to stagger home at 3:00
AM in the morning only to be confronted by your parent,
who promptly tell you how much of an idiot you are, lock
up all your video games and ground you for three months.

Or

…

You stagger home at 3:00 AM only to be confronted by
your parents, who have a sad look of disappointment on
their face. They tell you how disappointed they are and
that they expected so much more from you.

This analogy perfectly highlights how women feel in
relationships. The more her boyfriend attempts to control
her, the more she will slip through his fingers. She will
resist his control and proclaim her independence through
defying him. She does this to make a point: back off!

When your girlfriend does cross your boundaries, you
must be prepared to either tell her calmly that you find her
behaviour disappointing / unattractive, remove your
attention from her or follow through with an action of
some sort (breaking up with her in extreme cases such as
cheating).

Open boundaries are as close to "cheat-proofing" your relationship as you can get. Cheating is largely a form of rebellion; remove her desire to rebel and you remove the risk of her cheating.

BOUNDARY HIERARCHY

The "boundary hierarchy" resembles a ladder. Small boundaries start at the bottom while more significant boundaries reside at the very top.

Your Boundary Hierarchy may look something like the following:

- Cheating.
- Acting aloof.
- Lying to you.
- Being bossy.
- Being late.

Let your girlfriend cross a small boundary without consequences, and she'll keep pushing, further and further, until finally she's collapsed all boundaries and you are left standing alone, with no dignity. Every time she pushes past a boundary, she will lose respect for you. She must learn to respect your boundaries, for when she does, she will respect you as a man.

THE DIGNIFIED, SELF-RESPECTING MAN

It is the man who has integrity and self-respect that women want to stay and be with. Forever. In fact, when women play games with you and "test" your boundaries, they are really testing your sense of self-respect and integrity. Relationships are broken when women come to believe that their man values her over his own dignity and self-respect.

Setting boundaries is all about having respect for your own needs. Failure to respect your own wants and desires is a weakness. Women want to be with a man who will value himself just as much as he values her. There is no pedestal for the undeserving.

UNDERSTANDING BEHAVIOURAL PATTERNS

Negative patterns of behaviour are basically anything you let your girlfriend get away with that you would otherwise not do for somebody else. In the beginning of a relationship we tend to "put up" with much more than we are willing to maintain months down the road.

For this reason, it is far more effective to set your off-limit boundaries at the very beginning of your relationship. If you wouldn't put up with your girlfriend being late six months into your relationship, then don't put up with it one month in. Catch my drift?

Avoiding negative patterns of behaviour is absolutely critical when defending your boundaries. Once a negative pattern has been established, it is very hard to break. We, humans, are creatures of habit; we absolutely hate breaking a comfortable routine.

The boundary hierarchy must be defended the very moment you enter into a relationship. The standard must be set early on. Letting your girlfriend blatantly disrespect you will only cause a pattern of negative behaviour to form. She'll basically get used to you putting up with her crap, and expect that sort of compliance from you.

Once you finally clue into what's happening, you will

confront her about her rude behaviour, to no avail. She'll probably even laugh at you. You see, a negative pattern of behaviour has already been established and it will be an uphill battle to break out of it.

If you don't like going on fancy dates, then don't go on them at the very beginning of your relationship. It would be dishonest if you took your girl out four nights a week for three months, only to blatantly stop once the "honeymoon" period has ended.

If you like watching ESPN with your buddies on Saturday night, make sure you do so from the very beginning. Don't forego the things you enjoy in the beginning, only to re-establish them at a later date. When you try to reestablish a new pattern of behaviour, your girlfriend will interpret it as you losing interest in her. If you had set the precedent from the start, you wouldn't run into that problem.

It is because of these patterns of behaviour that I believe many of you will lose your current girlfriends. You will take my advice and become a more self-respecting, assertive man. You'll stop putting up with your girlfriends crap and most likely come on too strong and scare her away. It is important that you ease into applying the techniques in this book. Do not lay it all on her at once. This is especially true for those of you who are in current relationships where your girlfriend has all the power and control.

COMPENSATING GOOD BEHAVIOUR

INTRODUCTION TO REWARD/PUNISHMENT SYSTEM

What do you think most guys do when their girlfriend starts complaining (for no apparent logical reason) and bitching and blah… blah… blah… They respond with "Baby what did I do wrong? Here are some flowers to make things all better."

How long do you think it will take your girlfriend to realize that complaining, bitching and "blah, blah, blah" result in getting whatever it is she wants?

Bad behaviour = boyfriend getting me stuff…

We're doing the complete opposite of what we should, in fact, be doing. When she ignores us and plays the aloof game, or when she gets emotional for no reason, we will try to pull her in with affection because we ourselves want affection. At our core, we are being approval seeking. We want her love and affection.

REWARD GOOD BEHAVIOUR

Let's first focus on rewards, because I believe them to be the more important of the two. If you reward your girlfriend at the right time, she will not be giving you drama in the first place and thus you'll have very little need to punish her, in my experience.

Rewards are for the most part you giving her your validation and approval. You're not generically giving her gifts and complimenting her on this and that for no reason. Rather, you want to reward her efforts. This is the absolute best way to get your girlfriend contributing loads to the relationship. You need to reward the effort she puts in. Think about it; if you didn't reward her good behaviour, how would she know to continue doing all those good things that please you? Exactly, she simply wouldn't.

So how do you properly reward good behaviour? You simply tell her what you like. Plain and simple.

Let's say you love it when your girlfriend cooks for you, and you want her doing it more often because she makes the best. lasagna. ever. Simply tell her as you're eating: "Babe, you seriously have some killer lasagna making skills. Explain to me why you're not a chef again?"

Basically, you're giving her your stamp of approval. People love genuine praise and appreciation because they get so very little of it. The world is full of insecure, selfish individuals who only take their approval away.

Your girlfriend is no exception and you can bet she will eventually become addicted to your validation. She wants it and you will freely give it to her, provided she is doing good things for you, of course.

EXAMPLE GOOD BEHAVIOUR:

- Buying me something.

- Giving me really good sex.

- Cheering me up when I'm feeling down (emotional support).

- Driving me somewhere.

- Generally being an awesome girlfriend. You get the idea.

GIVING GIFTS AS REWARDS

Remember reading the section of this eBook entitled "The Most Important Thing About Relationships"? I taught you that when giving or doing anything for your girlfriend, you need to be doing it from the "right place". In other words, you can't be doing it to win her approval.

When I give gifts, I generally like them to be rewarded for good behaviour on my girlfriend's part. This way, my intentions can never be interpreted as approval seeking.

Once, my girlfriend gave me absolutely mind-blowing sex. It's usually pretty good as it is, but this one time, in particular, it was amazing. Naturally, the next day I drove over to the nearest flower shop and bought a few roses. I attached a card that said "These are for the AMAZING sex last night. You're awesome babe!"

That may sound a bit strange, but I can assure you that for the next few weeks, she tried extra hard to please me in bed. Point being let her know what you are rewarding, so she can do it over and over again.

Try your best to keep the gifts rare and meaningful. Put an emphasis on fun and not how much money you can blow on her. A playful fun night in the park is better than a $300 dinner. Most men don't consider nonmaterialistic things to be gifts when I believe they are the best gifts of all. You are giving her the gift of you.

A far better approach to gift giving is to invest your time and creativity into your gifts. It has the exact same effect as buying expensive material possessions, without looking like you're trying to buy her love or impress her.

Now, this isn't to say that all gifts have to be creative. In the example above, I simply bought flowers and it worked wonders. Mix it up a little and use your own

judgment. Just remember to always give your gift
(creative or otherwise) as a reward for positive behaviour.

58

DISCIPLINING POOR BEHAVIOUR

INTRODUCTION

Punish is a rather harsh word. There really is nothing harsh about what we are doing when we punish our girlfriend's bad behaviour. It needs to be done, not only out of love for ourselves but also out of love for her.

There are a number of ways to go about punishing your girlfriend, none of which involve getting angry, verbally abusive, manipulative or the like. In fact, those things come from a place of insecurity, which is not where we want to be coming from anyway. Even though anger as a form of punishment is far more effective than simply sucking up and doing nothing, there are even more effective ways to approach the matter.

The degree of punishment will largely depend on her behaviour and the boundaries you set at the beginning of your relationship. You'll be punishing your girlfriend for two main reasons: Her mood and negative actions.

REMOVING YOUR ATTENTION

When it comes to small things like bad moods, simply removing your attention and not actively feeding her bad mood is often enough. I know some guys who actually try to piss off their girlfriends when they are upset. I've had girlfriends do this to me as well.

When your woman is in a bad mood, it is generally a good idea to simply not be around her. Remove your attention from her as to not fall into her negative reality. Since your attention is a reward, removing it is a form of punishment.

Most of the time, her bad mood will have nothing to do with you. It's human nature to take out our bad moods on the people around us. Since your girlfriend is human (right?), she is no exception.

Removing your attention isn't just effective for mood swings either. It's effective for anything you don't like about her behaviour. Anything at all that you shouldn't be rewarding.

For example, some guys will cuddle with their girlfriends after being denied sex. They are effectively rewarding her (with cuddling) when they could be out doing other things they enjoy.

WARNING: Do not make it look as though you are removing your attention specifically to get what you really want. You should not pout or act offended in any way shape or form. You simply need to carry on your day in a regular, happy manner.

Removing your attention is not about ignoring your girlfriend. You should not ignore her. It is more about you simply not rewarding negative behaviour with mountains of attention.

DISAPPOINTMENT IS POWERFUL

So, what if your girlfriend does something? Let's say she starts playing jealousy games and flirting with other guys while you're around. Simply removing your attention from her will not make the problem go away in this case.

In this scenario, your best punishment would be to confront her with your disappointment. This is really where the "Kind but Firm" approach shines. Confront her in a cool, calm and collected manner. No anger or negative emotion.

I would say something along the following lines:

"You know, one of the reasons I like you so much is that you don't play silly jealousy games like all the other girls. But lately, it seems as though you have been and I have to admit that I expected more from you."

That's sure to put a stop to her games. She'll probably deny that it was her intention to play games and apologies, but it doesn't matter. Just give her a kiss on the forehead and say "Atta girl."

THE BIG STICK

Sometimes it will be necessary for you to bust out the "big stick". At some point, it will be required of you to put your foot down and make a tough decision. I've come to realize that in many cases you can either choose to lose your self-respect, or lose your girlfriend. I don't think at this point I need to tell you that choosing to honour your self-respect over your girlfriend is the way to go.

You need to be mentally prepared to tell your girlfriend to "get the fuck out of my house" and be prepared for her to actually leave forever. Don't even think about faking it either, because women can smell it when you're not sincere. You see, the funny thing is that if you're actually mentally prepared to let go of her, she is less likely to leave.

So, what type of behaviour warrants the "big stick"? Well, that really depends on your own personal values. It all depends on what you are not willing to tolerate; what your totally 100% off limit boundaries are.

For me, this would be the realm of cheating, lying about serious things, blatantly disrespectful behaviour, etc, etc. Serious things that go beyond her simply disappointing me.

(And just for the record, I refer to the "big stick" metaphorically and not literally. I don't literally mean take out a stick and hit anyone. That would be a cowards approach.)

SOME EXAMPLES

Scenario: Your girlfriend gives you the old "not tonight" routine.

THE WRONG WAY

You proceed to cuddle up and reward her negative behaviour with your affection. You fall asleep in each other's arms, even though cuddling isn't what you wanted.

THE RIGHT WAY

You simply remove your attention and affection from her and proceed to carry on with other activities. You are calm about her rejection and are careful not to come across as though you are intentionally shutting her out.

CONTROLLING DRAMA
A MAN ABOVE DRAMA

When it comes to dealing with drama, you must assume the attitude: "I am a mature man and am above all forms of childish drama". Once you truly own this attitude, you'll

notice that the women in your life no longer act bratty. This is a standard I set at the very beginning of every relationship I enter into. It doesn't take long for my girlfriend to figure out that I am a man above drama. She quickly follows my lead.

You need to act as though her being dramatic is ridiculous. If she were to start quacking like a chicken for absolutely no reason, how would you look at her? You'd look at her like she was nuts. That is exactly the look you need to give her when she starts acting dramatic. Just think of her quacking like a chicken.

Some relationship drama is inevitable. A handful of women are even completely addicted to drama while others are extremely laid back. Lots of drama is an off-limits boundary I set at the very beginning of my relationships. I simply do not tolerate it and I make this known by example. You must reinforce your relationships boundaries through clearly following through with the consequences to those set boundaries.

While simply looking at your girlfriend like she's nuts
will work in most cases sometimes you'll need to
actually say you think her behaviour is unattractive. This
is effective because women place a high value on their
appearance. Telling your girlfriend her bratty behaviour is
unattractive is about the equivalent of her telling you she
thinks you're weak and useless. Men place extreme
importance on being strong and useful.

Reverse the situation and put yourself in her shoes. Let's
say you were being a jerk to your girlfriend and promised
to take her to the moves that week. At the last minute,
you "forget" and hang out with your buddies, leaving her
hanging. What if she called you that night and told you
she thought you were useless and your wishy-washy
behaviour showed weakness and an inability to provide
for her. I bet that would make you want to redeem
yourself in her eyes.

The same psychology applies to her. She will
automatically begin to associate bratty behaviour with
unattractive appearance. That, along with the fact you
have the balls to tell her straight out what you feel, is very
powerful.

THE RULES OF ARGUING WITH WOMEN

Rule #1. Don't argue. "We're not arguing about this…"
is the best response you can give a short-tempered
girlfriend. If she is indeed trying to get across something
important to her, then talk about it in a mature manner.

If she's just bitching for the sake of bitch, get away from her and leave her vent on somebody else.

Rule #2. If you lose your cool, she wins. You need self-control when dealing with women and their emotions. You need to deal with everything in a cool, calm and collected manner.

Rule #3. Be open-minded. If your girlfriend genuinely has a good point, accept it. Don't be stubborn and "not give in" for the sake of not giving in. Be a man and admit when you are wrong or when your girlfriend has a valid point.

Rule #4. Empathize with the emotions she is feeling. Men always want to fix things when all they really need to do is say is "Yes, I understand you are feeling _ _ _ _ _ _." You hardly ever have to "fix" her problems. Just empathize with the emotion she is feeling at the moment.

HOW TO APOLOGISE WITHOUT BEGGING

FEELING AND EMOTION

Where will come a time when you honestly screw up and hurt your girlfriend's feelings. It will eventually happen at some point and when it does, don't assume it's supplicating to apologize. If you really did something

to genuinely hurt her, show that you're a quality guy and have no problem apologizing for the way you made her feel.

You simply need to apologize in the right way.

You need to apologize for the feeling and emotion you caused her. Only high-value people can affect others emotions. If you're not high value, she's simply not going to care. However, you are high value, so you assume you affected her emotions.

THE WRONG WAY:

YOU: "I'm sorry, I didn't mean to say that!"

The wrong way to apologize is to apologize for your actions.

THE RIGHT WAY:

YOU: "I'm sorry, I didn't mean to hurt your feelings."

Or you could drop the "I'm sorry" altogether and simply say: "I really didn't mean to hurt you. It wasn't my intention."

The more sincere you actually are when saying this, the more it will come through. That's a good thing.

APOLOGIZE WITH SELF-RESPECT

When you apologize from a position of weakness, you are doing so because of guilt, insecurity and ultimately fear. You need to first take a step back and accept that what you did was wrong and accept your own human shortcomings. You need to apologize as somebody with self-respect would apologize.

You see, women are literally programmed to seek out men who are mentally very strong. This is because it takes a strong leader to provide for any children you may have together. Even if you're both sterile, her genetic programming demands she seeks out men who exhibit masculine traits. When you start giving off signals of

weakness, this will ultimately kill any attraction she has
for you.

Apologize with the mindset "This has been a learning
experience for me and I'm ultimately glad that it
happened." This is exactly how a man with high self-
respect would apologize. Take heed.

KIND HOWEVER FIRM: FIGHTING RESOLUTION

The concept of "kind but firm" was introduced to me by an old girlfriend. She and I dated briefly; many, many years ago. We broke up and never really spoke to each other until years later while partying at a local club. Long story short: The next day we ended up having breakfast together and got onto the topic of relationships.

Now, it's been my experience that most women I talk with completely lacking any awareness of what they actually like in men. But not this girl. She was spilling everything and I was soaking in all that juicy relationship knowledge. The most interesting part of that knowledge was on her view of supplication (supplication = men acting like puppy dogs around women).

I told her that I had a problem: when I had a conflict with my girlfriend, I wanted to be a decent guy and avoid falling into the abusive asshole mode, but on the other hand, I didn't want to come across as a pushover, puppy dog man thing. She understood where I was coming from and gave me an amazing example of how to approach the situation.

She told me that she was planning on moving away from town only a few months back and that it would have meant leaving her boyfriend behind. She was dead set on moving.

She was sure he would get angry, upset and tell her how worthless she was, waste of time, etc. I mean, she was choosing a career over a man who loved her deeply, after all. Not exactly happy news.

To her surprise, he didn't get mad at all. In fact, he encouraged her! He said something to the effect of "Well babe, I think you're a wonderful girl and I care about you a lot, but if you feel as though this career is where you want to take your life, then I support you 100%."

Wow. She was totally taken off guard. Here was a guy who freely admitted to caring about her deeply, but at the same time, was totally willing to let her go. To let her be free.

He didn't respond in the typical way most men would have. Most guys would have either begged their true love to stay (the majority) or played a total aloof game of "I don't care, whatever bitch. Leave".

This guy was a
genius…

I thought about this newly discovered information for many days and loved how it fit in perfectly with my "complete freedom" approach to relationships. He was giving her complete freedom to do whatever she wanted to do. I will freely admit that prior to this revelation, I would have been the guy playing the aloof game. I would have more than likely given her a one-word response: "whatever". My bad.

Another (more clear) example of this system would be if your girlfriend starts disrespecting you (whatever that means to you). You could address the problem in the following manner:

"You know, one of the things I like and respect about you is that you're such a kind, sweet person. But lately, you've been pretty rude and disrespectful. I didn't expect that type of behaviour coming from you."

Basically, you want to calmly tell her that you admire x,y,z quality about her and then state what behaviour displeases you. You are being kind yet firm and there is no way this can be interpreted as insecure or needy, nor can it be taken as being rude. You are simply being mature about the matter.

LEAVING POWER

Too many guys are afraid of their own girlfriends. They are afraid that if they demand respect, they will lose them. It's funny and ironic how the opposite is actually true. To some

men, the fear of losing their girlfriend is literally crippling. Maybe you're even one of those guys. Regardless of what your answer is, you need to understand the concept of "walking power".

Understand that if a woman assumes that no matter how poorly she behaves, you will never leave her (walk away from her), she will continue to push your boundaries until they collapse. And as you now know, men without boundaries are very unattractive. She will leave you at that point.

This is why having solid boundaries is of the utmost importance. You need to be able to stand your ground and walk away from her if you must. I promise you that once she knows you are a guy with strong boundaries (which is what she wants in a guy), she will always respect you, with minimal "testing" on her part.

You cannot show your girlfriend that you are afraid to lose her. With that said, it's still perfectly fine (and required) to let her know you care about her. In fact, no relationship will last if she thinks she means nothing to you. What I'm saying is that you must not become so invested in her emotionally, that losing her would seem like the end of the world to you.

She needs to know that without her you would have no problem moving on with your life. Assume the attitude "I like you, but if we break up, it's not the end of the world."

When entering into a long-term relationship, you truly need to adopt a mindset that relationships are finite. Your relationship (in all probability) will not last until death due you part. Yes, it may, but approaching the relationship knowing things will not last forever, will actually help achieve the latter. Oh the irony.

Repeat after me: "If my girlfriend and I break up, sure I'll be sad because she's a great girl, we have fun together, but there are millions of women out there who I can have just as much fun with, if not more. If we break up, it will be an opportunity to explore other women."

SYMPTOMS SHE IS LOSING INTEREST

So how do you know when your girlfriend is losing interest in you? This is a question I often get asked by guys who have a gut "feeling" their girlfriend is just not into them as much anymore. It's been my personal experience that when I get this "gut feeling" I'm usually always 100% correct.

WATCH OUT FOR THE FOLLOWING:

Disqualifying herself. When an otherwise high self-esteem girl begins to disqualify herself. For example, she may say things like "I'm so fat, you shouldn't even like me" or "I suck at relationships. I'm just no good at them". Basically, she is trying to let you go without hurting your feelings. This behaviour only ends up hurting you more in the end.

Flirting. Excessively flirting with other men. This could be a sign she is "shopping around", although I've dated many women who are compulsive flirts and they really can't help it. I can relate to them as I myself flirt a bit more than I should while in a relationship.

Both women and men alike are validation junkies. Women (just like us men) will flirt to fulfil their sense of validation. If the otherer person flirts back, their sexual worth is somehow validated. Just because she occasionally flirts doesn't mean you should feel threatened.

Acting aloof. She doesn't call you as much anymore. She "forgets" about plans, you made together. She hangs out with "the girls" way too much.

Non-compliance. She no longer gives you compliance like she used to. Essentially, when a woman is really into her man, she will do pretty much anything for him. The less effort she is willing to invest in you, the less interested she is, in most cases.

Make sure to read over the chapter in this book titled "Let Her Invest in You". It's really something you should be doing from the the very beginning of your relationship.

Diminished Sex Drive. When your girlfriend gradually starts to lose all interest in sex, this is most likely a result of a lack of attraction for you. Her sex drive should be particularly strong during the "honeymoon" phase of the relationship. If she's really into you, she's going to want sex all the time for the first 4 – 6 months.

Monotone Voice. I've always said that a woman's vocal tonality is the key indicator of her current feelings and mood. When her voice is "girly", she is in a state of intense attraction. You will usually experience this directly after sex, in the "afterglow" period. To contrast, when a woman's voice is monotone and unimpressed sounding, she is sub communicating boredom and a lack of respect (and attraction) for you.

SEXUAL POWER

WOMEN LOVE SEX

The first realization you must make is that women want sex just as much as men. In fact, we humans are the only species on the face of this earth with an organ dedicated solely for sexual pleasure. It is the female clitoris. Recognize that this "magic button" has millions of nerve endings that provide women with orgasms ten times more powerful than our own. Jealous yet?

The problem with most guys is that they barely understand female psychology/ anatomy enough to satisfy her. I'm not saying this to make you feel inadequate by any means. This lack of understanding is the result of the fact men and women are for the most part wired differently. We men are primarily visual creatures, getting off on watching our girlfriends. Women, on the other hand, are emotional and derive pleasure from sounds, being dominated and touch. In short, the feelings they experience during sex are much more important.

One of the absolute best ways to get nonstop sex out of your girlfriend is to become a masterful lover. Becoming a quote "masterfull over" isn't even a particularly difficult thing to accomplish, and I will cover this very topic in a later section of this book. It really all comes down to understanding what women get off on. The answer is surprisingly very different than it is for us men.

Once you realize that you are doing women a favour by sleeping with them, your sex life will explode. She'll be the one wanting sex from you.

WARM HER UP

We men seem to think that "seduction" only occurs behind closed doors. Wrong! This is something I myself used to be particularly guilty of. You really need to start taking a more holistic approach to the seduction process. The bedroom is only one of the last "steps" if you will.

I'll share a personal story with you to better highlight my point:

My girlfriend and I were eating out one Saturday night. The food was good, conversation even better and the music definitely fit my taste. My girlfriend looked absolutely stunning to the point of me finding it hard to control my urges.

I leaned in, smiled, and whispered in her ear, "You look good. Just wait until you find out what I'm going to do to you tonight."

From that point on, I continued to hint around to what was to come later that night. This really got her warmed up (READ: horny), and as soon as we made it back to my place, she basically ripped my clothes off. I didn't have to make any "move" whatsoever since she was much hornier than I was.

You see, women need time to warm up, unlike us men. If we can just take the extra time to warm them up properly, the "seduction" has already been taken care of. We guys find this really hard to understand because we can rapidly become aroused within a matter of seconds. Women are not like this. It takes time and anticipation to warm them up.

SOUL GAZING ORGASM

As you're having sex with your girl and you can feel she is about to cum, command her to look into your eyes. It's been my personal experience that most women will not be able to hold eye contact for very long. Stop thrusting and command her again to look into your eyes. When she does, resume your motions.

This will cause her to have extremely powerful emotional orgasms. Orgasms she will enjoy immensely. It's also known as one of the absolute best ways to get her falling in love with you. Fast.

THE AFTERGLOW EFFECT

I've always said that the way to a women heart is through an orgasm. Sadly, the vast majority of men are missing out on a huge opportunity after the actual orgasm occurs. Women are literally in a state of perpetual bliss at this point. They are totally open to bonding and exchanging affections. This is the stuff love is made of guys.

You know how the old stereotype goes, where the guy just rolls over and falls asleep after robotically using his girlfriend as a masturbation toy. I hope that stereotype isn't actually true for any of you readers, but nevertheless, you can always do more when it comes to actually connecting with her after the sex is over. You know, when she wants to cuddle.

Use it as a time to talk, joke around and have fun. Much like when transitioning into a long-term relationship, you use this time to show her you want to take things to the next level. It doesn't end after the relationship has begun. Keep on doing it.

In fact, use this time to train her with your approval. Tell her that you love how affectionate she is, or how kind, or how appreciative etc, etc. Women are very receptive to this sort of thing directly after sex. I highly doubt there is a better time to affirm these qualities to her. Make her feel as though the qualities she possesses are rare, and you've hardly ever seen them in other women. If she feels special to possess them, she will fight long and hard to maintain that image in your mind.

DOING THINGS ON YOUR WAY

So, you want to be nice to your girlfriend while not coming across as overly submissive. No problem. Controlling your girlfriend's reality and maintaining power while still being a decent guy is actually not a hard thing to accomplish. The trick:

DO NICE THINGS FOR YOUR GIRLFRIEND ON YOUR OWN TERMS.

For example, if your girlfriend mentions that she likes a particular CD, you can randomly get it for her out of the blue. Women love surprises. Make sure to tie the gift in with some sort of reward for her good behaviour.

You can surprise her with a thoughtful email, card or even a small gift. As long as you're doing these nice things for your girlfriend on your own terms, and not because she pleaded or begged you to or because you want to win her approval. A big part of female romantic fantasy is having a man take charge and do things for her on his own terms.

Whatever you do, do not let your girlfriend negatively affect your reality. Do not appear angry, upset, sad or at all moved by anything she says or does. Just brush it off in a playful manner. Use the punishment/reward system we talked about earlier.

HOW TO AVOID LOOKING INSECURE

There are three main behaviours that make you look like an extremely immature, insecure guy. There is a lot of material floating around on the internet which encourages guys to erroneously engage in some of these behaviours. They don't help your cause one bit and only serve to lower your social status in the eyes of your girlfriend.

The bottom line is that these behaviours do not work while in a relationship. Period.

#1. Bragging

Everyone hates a bragger, yet we all do it more than we even realize. Bragging comes from a place of insecurity. When people brag, they intend to actually raise their social value by telling others how great they are. Ironically enough, this has the complete opposite effect. The person you brag to interprets this behaviour as approval seeking. Think back to a time somebody bragged to you. You probably just gave a polite smile and said something like "Oh, that's awesome dude". You interpreted their bragging as them trying to impress you.

As opposed to bragging, you should actively disqualify yourself. The power of properly implemented disqualification is simply amazing. Insecure people brag rock stars disqualify themselves.

#2. Putting Other People Down

I can't stand those who put others down. It smacks of the insecure bully in grade school who had to knock everyone down to make him/herself feel good. It may have worked for them in the 5th grade, but it will completely backfire when they reach adulthood. Putting other people down is a completely immature, insecure thing to do. Never do it. It conveys major insecurity.

#3. Putting Yourself Down

Once again, another insecure behaviour. Basically, you never want to go around feeling sorry for yourself. I mean, you obviously can and will at some point (you're only human after all). However, you don't want to convey that feeling to others.

Some guys will actually go on and on about how much they suck at this and suck at that. Stop doing that immediately! You're better than that. Women don't want to feel sorry for you; they want to be proud of their man and brag about him.

Bottom line: putting yourself down shows low self-esteem.

CIRCUMVENTING CHANGE

I've literally lost count of the number of guy friends I have who entered into a relationship only to be dumped a few weeks or months later. I'm sure if you think about it, you'll come to the

same conclusion. Maybe you've even been one of those guys. I certainly have.

The scenario is always the same. It starts off with the guy being really interesting, fun, adventurous, gives great sex, etc, etc. Then, slowly, he falls into a perpetual state of decline. Eventually, the couple is watching Family Guy reruns while munching on a TV dinner. Totally. Not. Fun.

Now, this book isn't about attracting women. Since you've already done that, I'm not going to give you any advice pertaining to "that part". But what I can tell you, however, is that whoever you were in the beginning of the relationship, is who you should be forever. This isn't something you can fake either. If you tried to fake it, you would only end up making yourself miserable. In fact, I can promise you that.

You may be able to put up a fake personality once a week at a local bar or club and get a one night stand, but you won't be able to maintain that personality forever. Like I said at the beginning, "inner game" becomes more and more significant the further your relationship progresses. She will eventually see the real you, so why not be proud of who you are, and show her from the very beginning? If she doesn't like you, well you've just filtered out another unsuitable chick. All the better.

This is why I say the selection process is so damn important. Take that section of this book seriously, for your own good. You really need to find a girl who likes your real personality and shares an interest in the things you take pleasure in. I cannot stress that enough. She doesn't have to like everything you do, but it'll totally save your relationship if you both share at least one passion. Snowboarding? Music? Whatever.

KEEP IT REAL

"Be yourself" is probably the best relationship advice your mom ever gave you. If you understand what it means. That mantra has been passed around from women to man for ages. The problem with it is that no man understands what it truly means! They think that women should accept their limited social savvy, bad body language, limited confidence and disgusting image. And if they don't, their bitches!

What women really mean by "be yourself" is to stop trying to impress them. The less you try to impress, the more attraction she will feel for you. That's what women have been trying to drill into our skulls for centuries. This is true both in side the context of a relationship and out.

I'm sure we've all been in the situation where we can feel our girlfriend slipping away from us. As males, we have

an inherent desire to take control of this seemingly
uncontrollable situation. An out of control relationship is
totally one of those situations. All of a sudden we change
our personality, we do everything she wants, etc.

Well, I hate to break it to you, but sucking up to your
women like that won't do you any good. Your
relationship problems stem from something other than
you not waiting on her hand and foot. I mean, you didn't
have to wait on her hand and foot in the beginning and she
still liked you. Look to the root of the problem and fix it.

Develop the traits of an attractive man.

THREE THINGS LADIES WANT FROM A RELATIONSHIP

FUN AND ADVENTURE

The song "girls just wanna have fun" really does ring true in so many ways. I put much emphasis on creativity and fun while in my relationships. Focus on having fun! It's not even just about her having fun; it's about you having fun and being comfortable with yourself. Remember: if you're having fun, she will also have fun by association. Never forget that.

It's important that you not approach your relationship with the mindset "how can I show my girlfriend a fun time?" Do whatever it is you enjoy in life, and take her along for the ride. Again, she will have a blast merely by association. It is imperative that you focus on having fun first and foremost.

Don't forget to check out chapter # at the end of this book. There you'll find tons of really interesting date ideas. You won't be running out of fun stuff to do with your girl any time in the next… you know… hundred years or so. Enjoy.

GREAT SEX

Great relationships are built on a foundation of great sex. I wasn't joking when I said women love sex just as much (and probably more) than men. Every time you make her orgasm, she is falling deeper and deeper in love with you. I mean that literally and not figuratively too. Women bond via orgasm. It's absolutely in your best interest to make her come as much as you possibly can.

At the end of this book, I've included many different sex tips and techniques that will get her coming every night. However, if you want to take it a step further (and you should) than I recommend anything by David Shade. This is who I personally learned from and I have a great deal of respect for the man.

EMOTIONAL SUPPORT

Be her emotional leader. Now, you don't have to get all sensitive and sappy if that's not what you're about. All you really need to do is listen. When women care about you, they will come to you with their problems. If you have a girlfriend, then you have a woman who cares about you.

Maybe she's not getting along with her parents. Maybe her dog died. Whatever. She's going to come to you and either cry or vent some steam. In most cases, all you need to do is listen. Don't even try to fix her problems. That's not what she wants you to do. As guys, we have this totally unnecessary urge to fix everything. Don't.

If you can actually relate to the problems she's having, do so. Tell her how you experienced the same thing and focus on the feelings you felt. Don't start giving her step by step directions on how to solve the problem; that's total bullshit and it won't help her. You need to relate to the feelings she's experiencing and just tell your story and let her relate back. No step by step instructions!

CHEATING

So what do you do if you end up cheating on your girlfriend? It's a valid question since we're all human and we make mistakes. Now, obviously, if you care about your girlfriend, you

shouldn't cheat on her in the first place. It's not something a responsible man would do. However, if it does indeed happen, there are definitely ways to admit to cheating and also ensure you keep your girl around.

When a man finds out his girlfriend just cheated on him, he will automatically want to know what it is she did with him, where he touched her and he'll generally make himself sick thinking about his girlfriend having sex with another man. We've all been there.

From an evolutionary perspective, this is a result of our need to "spread our seed". If we invest our time and recourses into a particular woman, we demand she be loyal (fair enough). Now, if another guy comes along and pokes his junk in her boom box, she can potentially get pregnant and we'll be stuck raising her children. Back in "cave man days", this was a very big deal because we would essentially be helping another man's genes survive while our own die off.

Now, with women, when they find out their boyfriend cheated on them, they will immediately ask "do you love her?" If they don't directly ask, they will be thinking it. They will generally make themselves sick thinking about all the romantic feelings you have for her. This is definitely in stark contrast to the above.

Women, unlike men, need to bear a child for nine months. If her man decides to split once he impregnates her, she's basically screwed. Well, at least in "cave man days" she would have been, as there would be nobody to provide for her and the baby.

For this very reason, it is absolutely essential that the women know her mate has a strong emotional bond (love) with her. If he does not, chances are, he won't stick around. Hence, women are more preoccupied with the emotional bond you have with them (or lack thereof).

Today, a woman can survive perfectly fine with or without a man to provide for her. Despite this, it is still in her genetic programming to think and behave in such ways. They cannot help it any more than you can.

So how does all this relate to you keeping your girl around after you've cheated on her? Simple. You need to emphasize the strong emotional bond you have with her. You need to make it abundantly clear that the emotional connection you have with her is stronger than it ever was.

I would say something along the following lines:

"I made a mistake. There was absolutely no emotional connection between me and her. I'm actually glad this happened because I realize now how strong our own connection really is."

Don't use the above as a script. Understand that you want to convey that there was no connection between you and the other women, while there is still a strong connection between you and your girlfriend.

I obviously can't promise you that this will work 100% of the time. Her trust in you will need repair and the only way to build trust is not to cheat on her again. Eventually, the trust she has for you will indeed return.

IF SHE CHEATS ON YOU

Next. Time to dump her faster than she can say "but honey it was an accident".

Alternatively, if you don't have a lot of emotion invested in your girlfriend, you can always tell her that you get a "freebie" and can choose another woman you want to have sex with. This will "even out the score". It may sound fair, but the freebie approach is not very wise. You might as well be in an open relationship if you're both going to be sleeping with random people. I don't even think I need to tell you to always wear a condom when having sex in this type of relationship.

In my opinion, it's best just to cut your losses and move on. There are better, more loyal women in the world. Think of it as a filter.

TRAINING HER WITH APPROVAL

Tell your girlfriend what you want her to be and she will become it. Okay, so I need to expand on that. If we flatter people with all the good things we think they are, they subconsciously have to become congruent with that perception whenever they are around you. If you tell your girlfriend you love how she is so appreciative and how no matter how trivial a thing you do for her she always says "thank you", she will have to conform to that perception you have of her.

If you have high expectations of your girlfriend, she will have to conform to those expectations. Do you act differently around your parents than you do around your boss? How about your best friend? Chances are, you act differently around each of them because they have a specific perception of you, in which you are subconsciously compelled to conform to. You may be an angel around your grandmother but a complete demon when around your friends.

I once had a girlfriend who after our first few dates always said "thank you" and showed appreciation for what I had done for her. It's my experience that women will usually always be appreciative on the first few dates, but gradually take you for granted over time. I'm generalizing of course, but this has been my personal experience.

Like in the example above, I told her very early on in the

dating process that I really respected how appreciative and thankful she always was. I told her that I found that particular quality in women to be rare and it made her special. Women absolutely love to feel special for genuine reasons (and this was a pretty genuine reason). From that point on, she always made an extra effort to say "thank you" no matter what I did for her. Even small little trivial things elicited a "thank you" response. I made sure to reaffirm this expectation I had of her every once in a while so she never forgot it.

I truly believe that we are what others expect us to be. Not just when it comes to relationships. Parents who have high expectations of their children end up having successful children. Likewise, the reverse is true. This is a proven fact.

WINNING HER DEVOTION

WORK IS GOOD

Tell me, why do you keep your sporting trophies on the mantel? Why didn't you throw away that stupid stuffed animal you won at the circus as a child?

Something can be utter and complete crap, but as long as you worked hard enough for it, you will place significant value on it. Its basic psychology: we value that which we have worked for. Although you're certainly not worthless (like some stupid stuffed animal) you can increase your perceived value tenfold by letting your girlfriend invest in you.

Simply put, the more time, energy and effort she puts into pleasing you, the more she will value you as a human being. You have truly become a prize, to which she has worked to obtain. For the same reason you can't seem to let go of your _, she won't be able to let go of you.

SMALL FAVORS

From a practical point of view, you can start by getting her to do small favours for you. Now, there is no reason to be an ass when getting her to do these things. For God's sake please don't start pouting for a glass of water every two seconds and make yourself look like some sort of I can't-do anything myself momma's boy. You simply can't be afraid to expect her to invest in you.

I know some guys who, when their girlfriends actually offer to do things for them, they quickly perk up and say "no no baby! It's fine, I'll do it!" As if letting their girlfriend do something for them would make them less of a man or something. Give me a break tough guy. She wants to invest in you, so let her! If your girlfriend ever offers to buy, pay or do something (within reason) for you, accept! Don't forget to say "thank you" and reward her with your approval either.

Some things you can get her to do for you:

- Write you a poem.

- Back massage.
- Hand massage.

- Any kind of massage.
- Surprise you with a gift.
- Wash your dishes.

- Wash your car.

- Clean your room/house.

Those are just some examples. Use your imagination and get her investing in you. She'll love you all the more for it, literally. My only word of caution is that you not go overboard. Like I said before, I don't want her waiting on you hand and foot like some mammas boy. Occasionally get her to invest in you. Start small and work your way up, until she's cleaning your place all to better please her man.

I highly recommend you start doing this from the very beginning of your relationship. Start small, and work your way up. If you've already established a pattern of negative compliance with your girlfriend, it can be difficult to put things back on the right track, which is why you will be doing yourself a huge favour to set up this behaviour at the very beginning.

THE "L" WORD

TO SAY IT OR NOT

The infamous "L" word has plagued many men with much torment and pain. "When should I tell her?" "Will she say it back?" "What should I do if she doesn't say it back to me?"

"How long should we be going out until I tell her?"

This is obviously an important point in any relationship. You're taking a big leap forward. If you tell her too soon, and she doesn't feel the same way about you, you risk creeping her out. She'll get scared and feel more than a little pressured to reciprocate.

All those daunting questions you have rolling around in your head can be circumvented if you would just let her worry about telling you she loves you. Much like letting the women advance casual sex into a long-term relationship, this is another area you need to let her worry about. Before you know it, on a starry, corny night she will be looking into your eyes and just blurt it out. It's funny because it will probably happen exactly like that. Stars and all.

Now, with all that said, there are still things you can do to let her know you care, without the implications and taboo "love" comes with. For example, you can say "I adore you". Saying this will also gently ease her into telling you she loves you since she'll more than likely know you'll say it back.

Also, when you're ready for it, tell her she's your best friend. I can't even begin to stress how amazing this is. If you really do feel as though you guys have progressed into becoming best friends, then tell her. Maybe after sex, while she's telling you how many orgasms you gave her, you could just hush her and say "You know what. You're my best friend". She may even break down into tears and start crying, so don't be surprised if that happens.

BE STRONG

You don't necessarily have to wait for your girlfriend to say "I love you" first. It's entirely possible she's thinking along the exact same lines as you. As always, you may need to lead her along, like the strong man you are. I don't want anyone interpreting this book as if it were some kind of bible. You need to learn how to use your own intuition above all else. So if your intuition is telling you that your girlfriend feels the same way, then it's probably time.

If you do plan on saying those three magic words (and that's perfectly fine), make sure they come from a place of strength. You're either telling her you love her in an approval-seeking way (because you want her to say it back), or you're saying it as if it were a favour from you to her. You can't expect her to give you the favour back.

If she doesn't say it back the first time, just remain strong in your conviction, and continue telling her you love her, without waiting for a response on her part. You're the big strong man and you'll say what you want when you want.

LOVE DOES NOT EQUAL NEEDINESS

Those who suffer rejection after rejection are conditioned over time to equate love with neediness. While it is correct that love can come from a needy, approval seeking a state of mind (one in which you only love to be loved in return), it is equally possible to love from a place of strength.

SPLITTING UP

INTRODUCTION

With the exception of those rare pathological nut jobs among us, breakups are hard. It doesn't matter if you're the one doing the heartbreaking or if you yourself are being given "the axe". It's hard stuff and there's no sense being ashamed of that. You're human and you have emotions so don't waste your time being needlessly insecure and afraid of that.

BREAKING UP WITH HER

Rule #1 is to be gentle. You don't like getting your ass dumped and neither does she. I mean, unless she cheated on you with your dad or something. Then, I can see why you might not want to take the "nice approach". You feel me, man?

Angry, hateful breakups are just not worth it. I can tell you that from personal experience. Emotionally, there will always be regret, especially if you both end up saying things you don't mean. It will be hard to form any sort of friendship after the fact if you part on bitter, angry terms.

Be clear. Don't muddle your words with "I think" and "maybe we should". Instead, you have to MAN UP and be crystal clear. You tell her you're through.

- It's over.

- We're breaking up.

- We're through and you're not my girlfriend anymore.

Leave not a shadow of a doubt in her mind.

Be concise. Do not draw things out any more than they have to be drawn out. The sooner you get through with the breaking up part, the sooner you can both move on with your lives.

Break up in person. Be a man about the matter and do it in person. I don't care if you were going out for just two months, always do it in person. Under no circumstances whatsoever should you ever break up through email, text message or similar. That's totally not a classy move on your part. MAN UP and do it in person.

Break up in public. Go out for coffee, do it in a food court, wherever. This will prevent any dramatic outbursts on her part. And make sure it's a place you can easily leave just in case she does decide to make a dramatic scene.

No clichés, please. Don't bother saying stuff like "it's not you it's me" or "you're too good for me, you deserve somebody better". You owe her an honest explanation. Leave it to women to use all the clichés. You're a man and you will break up with her like a real man would.

Don't place blame. Avoid blatantly placing any blame. Unless you want an all-out argument to ensue that is…

Be honest. Give her an accurate depiction of why you are really breaking it off with her. Does she lie about the most ridiculous things? Are you no longer attracted to her physically? Just be honest and tell her. If the situation was reversed and she was breaking up with you, I'm sure you would want to know exactly why.

The line that works every time: "We're just not compatible." You can modify it as long as the basic premise is there. You're not placing blame, she can't argue your point, etc. It's truly the best breakup line ever devised.

WHEN YOU GET DUMPED

Getting dumped by your girl is never fun, but it's happened to us all so remember we've all been there.

Break off contact. If you still have feelings for the girl, break off all contact. You don't have to be immature about it or anything. Just tell her you have other plans if she ever calls and asks you to hang out with her. You two may end up sleeping together again (very probable) and that is not something you want. You want to get over this chick and get over her fast.

Get a life. Go out with your buds as much as possible. Focus exclusively on having as much fun as you possibly can. This will help you get your mind off her.

Get a rebound. You won't hear any other relationship book give this advice! Rebounding does work, especially if you're self-esteem is left a bit jaded after the breakup. Obviously, you don't want to get into a cycle of sleeping with women only as a means to validate your self-worth. Be mature about your rebound and never lead any of the women on. Be clear that it's casual sex only.

Don't check profiles. Don't you dare check her social networking profiles such as Twitter or Facebook? Stay the hell away from any of her personal pages. She's going to have guys posting messages to her (very blatantly flirtatious massages) and probably even posting blog notes about her love life. She'll even be adding pictures of her out partying with other guys. Women are very savvy when it comes to creating jealousy.

If you want, you can use these sites to your advantage by actively (and publicly) flirting with other women. This will help you move on with your life and it'll boost your confidence. I can guarantee you that your ex will be viewing your profile. Whatever you do, don't make it look obvious that you're trying to make her jealous (if that is indeed what you are doing). Your effort will go in vain if she knows you're doing it to upset her. I recommend you just move on with your life and don't even bother trying to my her jealous.

DIVERSE RELATIONSHIP TIPS

MOVING IN TOGETHER

Yet another giant leap, deeper and deeper into your relationship. I generally consider it a bad decision for you to be the one moving into your girlfriend's place. You want her either moving into a house/apartment you both agree

upon or preferably moving into your place.

From a psychological point of view, if you move into your girlfriend's place, it's still hers. She still owns the territory, even if you assume

100% of the rent. No matter what, you will always be a guest in her home. Although it's not the end of the world, I highly recommend she move into your place. It will save you more than a few headaches, guaranteed.

DRESS IT UP, BABY!

Yes, you may be insanely attracted to your girl now, but eventually, you will grow desensitized to that pretty little face of hers. She'll become a little boring to you, and you'll become a little boring to her. Fortunately, there is a way to cheat this eventuality.

Get her to put on a wig. Seriously. It's totally that simple.

I don't know if you've ever seen a long-term girlfriend put a wig on (blue is my favourite) but I can assure you you'll want to jump her bones immediately. It's almost as though she's just turned into another person.

FORGET ABOUT VALENTINES DAY

It's time to say goodbye to good ole' Valentine's Day. Why? Because it conditions us to believe that gifts are only reserved for special occasions when they're not. When you give a gift on Valentines Day, it's out of necessity and little else. It's not a reward for the good behaviour your girlfriend has been showing you; it's simply because society says you have to.

If you're already in a relationship and have already shared Valentines Day together, it's not easy to just call it quits. You've established a pattern of behaviour which is not easy to break. Your best approach is to sit down with her and explain your new views on the matter. Tell her how you believe Valentines to be over-commercialized and that when you buy her a gift, you would rather it be for a reason (and thus have meaning), as opposed to society dictating that you have to.

TECHNIQUES TO BEAT PREMATURE EJACULATION

Reaching orgasm too soon during sex is embarrassing. You don't need me to tell you that. You want to be able to please your partner or you fear she may leave you in search of a

better mate – who will please her properly. Stop worrying my friend, because when finished reading this article I assure you, you'll have a clear understanding not only of what causes your premature ejaculation but 5 practical techniques for overcoming this relatively common problem.

According to recent studies, premature ejaculation affects 25 to 40% of all men. That number is actually much higher in younger men aged 18 – 30. In the 18 – 30-year-old age group, the median time until orgasm is between 6 and 8 minutes. That's definitely not long enough to bring the average women successfully to orgasm. Believe me.

In fact, most men consider themselves premature ejaculators when they cum before their partner reaches orgasm. I would tend to agree with this, but keep in mind that some women find it hard to orgasm, even if you last 30 minutes. A few women are actually cursed with this problem, so don't be too hard on yourself if you can't please this type of women. It's really not your fault.

Technique #1 – Mental Distraction

The mechanism related to orgasm is largely thought to be psychological. Basically, the more aroused you are, the faster you will reach orgasm and cum. In order to decrease your state of arousal (and thus prolong your orgasm), you must actually mentally distract yourself from the act of sex.

One such way is to think about distasteful things. For example, if you feel yourself reaching orgasm, think about dirty socks. I remember the last time I was having sex with my girlfriend, I felt myself reaching orgasm before I had properly satisfied her, so I noticed a pair of dirty socks lying on the bottom of the bed. I concentrated on how gross I thought they were, and suddenly I could no longer feel myself climaxing. This is a very simple and effective technique.

Another example could be to think of something you find physically unattractive about your partner. You may find that extra roll on her tummy more than a little distasteful – so think about it! Think about how it grosses you out and before long you'll notice you no longer feel like climaxing. Mission accomplished my friend.

The downside to this technique is that it will only work temporarily. Personally, I can only think about dirty socks a few times before I subconsciously start to ignore those thoughts. So I have to switch it up every now and then and focus on different things. So I'm continuously thinking of new things to distract my mind. As a result, this technique is best used in the short term and in combination with the other techniques I have listed below.

Technique #2 – Mild Pain

A variation of the above technique (but warranted of its own category) is to inflict mild pain upon yourself. No, I'm not a sadist thank you very much. This is actually a very effective form of mental distraction. It works like a charm.

So what do I consider "mild pain"? Well, you could try lightly biting your lip or the inside of your cheek. You could pinch yourself or even get your partner to pinch you. Where you pinch yourself is up to you. I'll just stop myself there.

Technique #3 – Masturbation

Masturbation before sex can help you last longer in bed. Basically, after you've already ejaculated, it becomes harder for your body to become fully aroused quickly. You'll last much longer if you can masturbate a few hours before sex. However, this is obviously problematic if the sex is unplanned. Thus, if you know you'll be having sex with your partner in advance, keep in mind that it will help you last longer if you masturbate first.

Furthermore, I must caution that you shouldn't overly rely on this technique. Premature ejaculation has a lot to do with performance anxiety, so if you happen to overly rely on this technique, you run the risk of increasing your anxiety when you happen to not masturbate before sex one time. This article contains a great number of practical, useful techniques you can use. There is really no need for you to overly rely on only this one technique. You have lots to choose from here!

Technique #4 – Pace Your Breathing

Ever notice that once you start to reach orgasm, your breathing increases to a rapid pace? When you start out, your breathing is slow and steady, but as you continue thrusting, your breathing increases until finally you orgasm and your breathing return to normal. It's been proven that the pace of your breathing is related to your ability to climax.

You need to make the pace of your breathing slower and steadier. Pace yourself and prevent breathing too rapidly. This will dramatically improve the time you last in bed. It also has the added benefit of distracting you mentally, since you're concentrating on something other than sex, which as you already know increases your "lasting power".

Technique #5 – Relax Your Pubococcygeus Muscle

Your pubococcygeus is the muscle around your penis. You know when you have to pee really badly and there is no bathroom around? Well, the muscle you're using to hold it in is your pubococcygeus muscle. The same thing applies to when you're actually peeing and you suddenly try to stop and hold it in. Yeah, well that's the muscle I'm talking about.

Now that you understand what it is I'm talking about, I want you to completely relax that muscle the next time you're having sex. If you're anything like me, you have a nasty habit of tensing that particular muscle up during sex. Believe it or not, relaxing it can help you last longer in bed.

TECHNIQUES FOR DELIVERING INTENSE ORGASMS

Oral Sex "Cough Drop" Technique

This is an oral sex technique for you to use on your girlfriend or wife. It's very simple to perform and yet extremely pleasuring at the same time. Your partner will go absolutely wild over it!

YOU NEED:

1. A mentholated cough drop. (just one)

The idea behind this technique is basically to put a cough drop in your mouth, suck on it for a few minutes until it dissolves and then go down and perform your duties as you normally would (giving your partner oral sex). Apparently different cough drop flavours provide a diverse array of pleasurable sensations. It's really a matter of personal preference on the woman's part, so make sure you try a number of different flavours.

Let the cough drop swirl around in your mouth. While you wait for the cough drop to dissolve, you can take this time to TEASE your lover. Kiss her bikini line, her nipples, blow gently in her ear, whisper to her what you plan on doing. Make her WAIT in anticipation for what you are about to do to her. She'll love you for it.

Once the cough drop has dissolved, go to work and perform oral sex on your lover. Make sure to focus on mostly licking her clitoris. To absolutely make her go completely wild, stop every once in a while (only a few times) and gently blow on her clitoris. The air will react with the menthol, creating an amazing sensation for your lover.

When you're finished working your magic, ask for her input on how mind-numbing the experience was. Try to figure out what cough drop flavour elicits the most intense, mind-numbing orgasms. Note that you can also tell how much she likes it through listening to her moans.

Oral Sex – "The Corkscrew"

All you need to perform this awesome technique is your hand. That's it!

Have your woman lie on her back with her knees bent and her legs open wide. Now sit in between her legs as though you were about to give her oral sex. Cross your fingers (index and middle finger) and insert them into her vagina.

Slowly rotate your forearm back and forth. Gradually go deep enough so your thumb is eventually brushing up against her clitoris.

Continue rotating your crossed fingers back and forth until she has an explosive orgasm.

Oral Sex – Ice Cube Pleasure

The "Ice Cube Erection" oral sex technique is a classic, and one I'm proud to say I personally used to use even before I knew it was a "classic". Your women will absolutely go wild for this. Remember that the number one way to have consistent sex is to actually have the skill to pleasure your partner and give her mind-numbing orgasms. If you can achieve that (with my help) I can guarantee you'll be getting loads more sex for yourself. What guy wouldn't want that?

Enough with the hype. Let me teach you this amazingly powerful technique.

Get your girl naked and lying in your bed.

Get yourself a normal ice cube from the fridge (you can also experiment with freezies as well). Put it in your mouth and let it melt a tiny bit. Next, bring the ice cube to the front of your mouth and hover over your girl, letting the ice cube drip on your partner's nipple. Her nipple will almost instantly become completely erect. Make sure you move on to the next nipple, dripping a few more drops of liquid ice onto it until it is completely erect.

Now for the best part:

Rub the tip of your tongue onto the ice cube until it's very cold. Now, begin performing oral sex on your partner. Make sure you focus mainly on her clitoris. Only an armature will venture from the clitoris for very long. Make sure you continue to rub your tongue on the ice cube every few minutes when you feel your tongue getting hot. As you have already undoubtedly figured out, the pleasure within this technique is derived mainly from the cold sensation of the ice cube.

Oral Sex – "Panty Buzz" Technique

The simple act of reading this short article will probably get you off – imagine what will happen once you actually perform it. The "Cotton Panty Buzz" technique will have your women begging you for more sex, night after night. Remember, the better you can please your women, the more sex you'll be getting. She'll eventually be begging you.

Enough with the hype. Allow me to teach you!

You'll Need:

1. Pair of cotton panties

2. Bottle of wine

Have your partner wear the panties and remove the rest of her clothes. Hell, get her to do a strip tease for you if you're feeling adventurous. Be creative and use your imagination.

Next, have your partner stand, while you kneel in front of her. Slowly feel up her inner thighs, gently massaging them and licking around her bikini line. Whatever you do, don't touch her clitoris. There will be plenty of time for that later. For now, you want to tease her. Women love being teased; they like it far more than us guys do.

After teasing her for a few minutes (two is enough) pull the waistline of her panties toward you. Pour a bit of the wine into her panties and release your grip on the waistline. Allow the liquid to soak itself into your partner's vagina and her cotton panties.

After a few seconds or so, begin to suck on her crotch. Suck in all the wine, drinking it in the process. Your partner will most likely begin to squirm around, thrusting her crotch in your face. This is a good thing, as it means she is becoming extremely horny.

Continue repeating this process two or three more times until you're ready to either give your partner oral sex or have sex with her. Trust me when I say she'll be more than ready to have sex with you!

CRUCIAL LIST OF ROMANTIC IDEAS

Name a star after her. Surf on over to Star Registry and sign up for one of their various packages. If you go with the custom package, you'll receive a 16" X 12" full-color parchment certificate personalized with the star name, date and coordinates. You will also receive a personalized 16" X 12" sky chart containing the star name, star date, the constellation and the location circled in red where the star is in the sky. It will cost you around £40 ($54) + S&H.

Get her a newspaper that was published on her birthday. There is actually a site called Newspaper Archive that does this. Go there and click on "Birthday Newspaper", find the date she was born and have it shipped to you. The cost of this will run you 29.95 + S&H.

Send a postcard with a note on the back. It could say something like

"for being such an awesome girlfriend".

Mail a poem or letter to her.

Design a small web page for her if you know how. I did this and made sure to tease her with a lot of inside jokes we had between the two of us. You could also register a Wordpress account and design something around that.

Make sure you stay away from strictly cheesy, sappy love stuff. I like to mix in a lot of teasing with a bit of cheese for the best effect.

Send her flowers. Not creative at all but it always works. Don't forget to put a nice little message on the card that comes with the flowers.

THE ULTIMATE LIST OF DATING VENUES

T he following is a list of really interesting date ideas. Too many guys fall into a boring, predictable pattern of either watching reruns of family guy with their girlfriend every

weekend, or taking them out for dinner constantly (not to say dinner dates are bad, just don't be doing it all the bloody time!) This list will give you fun and interesting things to do together for literally all of eternity.

Dance Lessons

Art Classes / Lessons

Clay Pottery Lessons

Water Balloon Fight

Lazer Tag

Hiking

Cook Dinner Together

Play Board Games

Sunset Picnic

People Watching

Shopping

Ice Cream

Judging Wine Tasting

Painting Class

Rock Climbing

Planetarium

Science Museum

Kite Building

Ice Skating Skiing / Snowboarding Bike
Riding

Zoo

Arcade

Vintage Clothing Store

Jet Skiing Boating

Sailing

Play Frisbee in Park

Skydiving

SUMMARY

An now that's it! You should now feel you have the all the knowledge and skills needed to take back control of your relationship and keep it! Or just be able to mould that certain someone into the perfect obedient girlfriend. Sure, they'll be some bumps along the way! There are no quick fixes in life but within everything you've just read is the bones for a perfect relationship!

Lastly a huge thank you to for you the reader for purchasing this book and taking the time to read it! We are dedicated to making the most enriching learning experiences for you the reader and hope you have as much fun using your newly found skills and techniques as having in researching and creating this book!

THE ULTIMATE GUIDE

HOW TO TRIAN YOUR GIRLFRIEND

www.ingramcontent.com/pod-product-compliance
Lightning Source LLC
Chambersburg PA
CBHW070807260726
48660CB00005B/1748